How
to
Network

Networking Tips for Solopreneurs and Self-Employed Consultants

Heidi Thorne

First Edition, February 2016

Thorne Communications LLC, USA
www.ThorneCommunications.com

How
to
Network

Networking Tips for Solopreneurs and
Self-Employed Consultants

Heidi Thorne

Table of Contents

It Started with a Postcard...

One day several years ago, I received a handwritten postcard in the snail mail from an accountant friend inviting me to visit a networking event as her guest. At that time, I was pumping up some different profit centers in my business. So I figured, "Why not?"

I wasn't sure what to expect. When I arrived, there were maybe a dozen or so people, who seemed to all know each other, chatting away while they munched on some breakfast. Then the official meeting started and followed a pretty strict agenda with some administrative updates, everyone having a bit of a presentation, and a featured presentation of maybe 10 minutes. The point of the meeting was to keep these people connected with each other for the purpose of building their own and the groups' businesses by passing referrals. This was my first experience with a leads group, a very specific type of networking experience.

After that initial meeting, I joined, embraced the concept and the group, and became president of the chapter not too long afterward when a vacancy occurred. It was life changing and challenging, and I am forever grateful for the friendships and support I received.

But a couple years into my leads group experience, one of the chapter's members and I met up for coffee. He was getting a bit weary of the group and was looking into more networking opportunities with the new (at that time) social media channels. As he talked, I had one of those epiphany moments since I realized that I, too, was getting weary of struggling to dig up leads for other members, getting a less than expected ROI, all the while investing heavily in terms of both time and money. Not too long afterwards, I moved on.

Since then, I've actively participated in just about every type of networking venue possible: chambers of commerce, other leads groups, Meetup groups, business events and seminars, social media, online chats, nonprofit volunteering, speaking engagements, webinars... you name it. For a time, I had a reputation of "being everywhere." But omnipresence has its drawbacks. (I think God would agree.) Once again, I was getting weary and frustrated. I knew I needed to figure out this networking nonsense. I hired a business coach and had more epiphany moments that helped me get back my life and be much more efficient and effective when it comes to making connections to build my business.

My hope in sharing my experience is to help you think more like a boss, making informed and strategic decisions when it comes to evaluating networking opportunities... even if you're just the boss of your own one-person empire.

If, after reading this book, you're still swirling in a business building blur, connect with me at HeidiThorne.com and let's discuss how coaching with me might help you get off the networking treadmill and take some real steps forward.

Let's get working on your network!
Heidi Thorne

NETWORKING BASICS

CHAPTER 1:
What is Networking?

The One Business Skill They Typically Don't Teach In College

What's the one critical skill that is almost never taught in college, even business school? Networking. Yet, without it, one's career can easily be a non-starter.

Even worse is that many people have an *"I know it when I see it"* attitude when it comes to networking. But without a clear understanding of what it exactly is and how to use it, connection activities can be a frustrating and futile exercise.

Networking Definition

While the dictionary may have an official definition for it, here is my functional definition of networking in business:

Networking is the process of establishing and maintaining connections with groups of individuals for the purpose of mutual support.

The two pillars of the networking process are **establishing and maintaining connections** and **mutual support**.

Establishing and Maintaining Networking Connections

This is at the heart of the networking process. Establishing connections can be done in a variety of ways and venues. But the most common method for business is through participation in networking groups. These groups can include:

- *Chambers of commerce*
- *Leads groups (BNI, Le Tip, etc.)*
- *Associations and clubs*
- *Networking events*
- *Social networking via social media and other online venues*
- *Informal networks of friends, family, colleagues and vendors*

The key is to participate in the right groups because not all networking groups are created equal in terms of their ability to reach the people you want to reach.

And like groups, not all connections are ideal connections. Agreed, following a "you don't know who they know" philosophy, even irrelevant contacts can often come up with some outstanding referrals. But the cost in terms of time and effort to maintain and grow connections with people far removed from your target audience can be counterproductive.

Remember, also, that a "like attracts like" principle is also at work. Even if the ideal prospects you are directly connecting with in these groups do not become buyers, they may be able to refer you to people just like themselves who may be a good fit for you.

So the point is to evaluate networking groups and opportunities based on their ability to connect you with a big enough pool of people from the market segments you want to reach.

Networking is a long-term investment. It takes a significant amount of time to attend networking groups and events, follow up with good connections (via email, phone and in-person meetings) and maintain a presence in that arena until even a first sale is made. This could be months or even years, depending on the type of networking done and what is being sold.

Mutual Support

Networking is a dance of giving and getting. Networkers who participate only to get are usually obvious and are usually gone quickly. On the opposite side of the spectrum, network members who give too much (for example, volunteering for every possible committee) are also gone quickly due to burnout.

Decide how much time, effort and dollars you can and are willing to invest in each particular network in order to achieve your business goals while providing support for fellow members. Remember that the goal is mutual support.

Support can take the form of:

- *Buying needed products and services from network members. The emphasis is on "needed." No pity buys!*
- *Giving relevant referrals to others.*
- *Participating in meetings, events and special projects.*

Heidi Thorne

But Isn't Networking the Same as Word of Mouth?

No! Though both networking and word of mouth advertising seek to share connections and information with people one knows, they are completely different in terms of their goals and function. An example will better illustrate.

Say that I visit a new restaurant in town and I tell my neighbor about my great experience there. That's word of mouth. On the other hand, say I have a conversation with the new restaurant owner while I'm dining and I learn that he needs help with his marketing. I then refer him to a marketing consultant friend of mine. I have an established relationship with the marketing consultant and am looking out for her interests, as well as the interests of the new restaurant owner connection I just made. That's networking.

Word of mouth is completely noncommittal. I don't honestly care if my neighbor actually visits the new restaurant in the example or not. And the restaurant owner has no idea if I will, or will not, share information about his place with anyone.

Networking has some level of investment on the part of all parties. In the example, I had to strike up a conversation with the restaurant owner. I also had to already have the established connection with my marketing consultant friend and had to take time and effort to connect her with the restaurant owner. So what's in it for me? I'll have made this connection in the hopes that when they see an opportunity that's suitable for my business, they'll reciprocate and connect me.

6

CHAPTER 2:
Types of Business Networking Groups

Not All Networking Groups are Created Equal

When it comes to networking groups, they are definitely not all the same. Nor are they all equal in terms of the sales and referral opportunities they offer.

Below some of the most common networking groups are reviewed, with pros and cons for each.

Chambers of Commerce

This is the classic networking venue for local and small businesses. A chamber of commerce is an association made up of paying members located within or near the geographical area the chamber serves. Being able to identify one's business as a member sends a message to locals that the business is committed to the community.

Chamber events are designed to help members make connections, build relationships and facilitate sales among members. Typically, chamber meetings and events are open to members only. Visitors may only be allowed to participate in certain events or a limited number of events before they are asked to make a decision about their commitment to join. Some chambers may be more inclusive of visitors and merely charge them higher event admission fees.

PROS

• *Builds a sense of community and friendship.*

• *Gives members a recognized positive status in the community with both consumers and fellow businesses.*

CONS

• *Limited exposure due to emphasis on immediate geographic community.*

• *May have less appeal for younger generations who network primarily online and with social media, as well as businesses of all sizes with national or international clientele.*

• *Some chambers may have high numbers of very small businesses which have limited buying power for doing business with other members.*

Leads Groups

Of the networking categories, leads groups are the most hardcore due to a high level of financial, time and effort investment. However, for some businesses, they can be very effective if the group is a good fit.

Popular leads group organizations include BNI (Business Network International), Le Tip and a host of other regional, national, international and special interest organizations (i.e., women only leads groups). Some chambers of commerce also have subgroups that operate as leads groups.

In these organizations, the meetings are structured and every chapter follows the same meeting agenda and procedures. The point of these groups is that each member is required to bring genuine quality leads and referrals for other chapter members. Chapters may also be subdivided into referral partner subgroups who have similar clients, thereby facilitating lead and referral flow.

PROS

- *The high level of investment can weed out less serious networkers, thereby offering members a pool of more committed referral partners.*
- *Highly structured meetings give everyone equal opportunity for participation and exposure within the group.*
- *Ideally, members hope that if they pass along quality referrals and leads it will result in them receiving the same from other members.*

CONS

- *Like chambers of commerce, leads groups have been challenged by social media, the Internet and population shifts toward younger, more digitally savvy individuals.*
- *Also, like chambers, the exposure may be limited to local businesses. As well, the size of the chapter groups can be smaller and the mix of people may become static.*
- *Unfortunately, not all members may be willing or able to bring quality referrals to other members and/or only bring business to a few of the chapter's members. This can lead to disappointment, resentment and eventual member dropout.*

Because of their high investment and more complex structure, leads groups will be discussed in more depth in a following chapter.

Networking Events

Other than formal and regularly scheduled meetings and events such as those in chambers or leads groups, one-off trade shows, events, workshops, seminars and conferences can offer quality networking opportunities.

PROS

- *Attendees are drawn to events due to common interests which can foster quality and relevant connections.*
- *Events limit time spent networking to the event period and whatever follow up time is needed. No regular meeting commitment is required.*

CONS

- *Because the time spent at these events is limited, post-event connections can quickly evaporate if proper follow up is not done.*
- *Depending on the event and the venue, expense can be a factor.*

Associations

Associations are groups that come together based on some mutual interest or qualification. Examples would include: industry, gender exclusive (women's networking groups are popular), age, hobbies, charitable support, education, alumni status or profession (i.e., HR managers).

Associations organized to band together people who are in the same type of business, profession or industry are essentially made up of competitors. Networking with competitors? Yes! And while that must be done without sharing confidential or proprietary information, having a network of supportive friends and colleagues in one's same line of work can be helpful should the occasion arise where an inappropriate piece of business must be referred elsewhere. Additionally, these associations usually have members who support or supply the industry which can be helpful resources.

PROS

- *Collegial relationships within the group can foster unity and mutual support.*
- *It can be very reassuring to have a list of competent fellow competitors who can assist with overflow or inappropriate sales leads.*
- *May provide connections for new career opportunities.*

CONS

- *Distrust of competitor members can create adversarial relationships which can damage an industry.*
- *One must be careful not to share confidential or proprietary information with competitors.*

Social Networking

Sure, all networking groups are social! But in today's terms, social networking usually refers to activities on social media. This can take the form of hashtag communities,. forums, online chats, groups and more.

Hybrid groups, such as those on Meetup.com, combine social networking aspects with in-person meetings.

PROS

- *Could expand sales territory to a worldwide audience.*
- *Offers the opportunity to get to know new prospects with little dollar investment and in a (usually) friendly environment.*
- *The loose structure and churn of participants can keep these networks fresh and dynamic.*

CONS

- *The barriers to entry for social networking are so low that it can attract a wide variety of unsuitable, but friendly, connections that waste time.*
- *The level of commitment to these social networks is also so low that it is not uncommon to have participants leave the group almost as soon as they join it.*
- *Time invested in active participation can span hours which could be more productively be spent in other venues.*
- *Personal security issues can be a concern since there are those who prey on unsuspecting individuals. Care must be exercised to not share too much or too personal of information on social networks to protect privacy and safety.*

Informal Networks

Each one of us can have a personal network ranging into the hundreds (thousands?) of connections of friends, neighbors, acquaintances, family, vendors, clients, etc. that can help build a business network. While these do not require regular meetings, connections can be very powerful due to personal association.

PROS

- *No formal meetings or specific dollar investment required!*
- *Due to personal connection, relationships can be fulfilling and productive.*

CONS

- *There is no requirement to share members of one's personal network with anyone... and many people don't!*
- *Should a connection between members of one's informal network go bad, it can have lasting negative effects on a close relationship.*

CHAPTER 3:
What is a Leads Group?

A leads group (sometimes called a leads club) is a business association whose members gather on a regular basis (typically weekly) for the purpose of giving and getting referrals. Some of the popular associations include BNI (Business Network International), Le Tip, leads groups sponsored by chambers of commerce, and groups for special audiences (i.e. women-only leads groups). Larger national and international associations usually have one or many chapters within a given region or metropolitan area.

Typically, annual membership dues are assessed to cover administrative costs (meeting room fees, website costs, etc.) and gain membership privileges. In addition to the membership dues, a meal fee may be required for any food and beverage consumed at each meeting. The meal fee may be a set fee or may only be assessed for menu items ordered.

Meetings are structured to give fair exposure to all members in the group. The meetings usually include an open networking period followed by a structured agenda that includes introductions, group administrative matters, education, testimonials and, of course, passing of leads and referrals. There may be a referral quota required of each member per meeting.

One of the primary benefits of leads groups for networking is exclusivity. In other words, once a membership is secured, it bars someone else in the same profession from joining the group. This gives members a competitive advantage over non-members.

Attendance is required, though a limited number of absences may be allowed. When a member will miss a meeting, he or she may be allowed to send a substitute to represent him or her for that day. Substitutes usually cannot promote their own businesses during meeting, but may be allowed to connect with members during certain periods (i.e., open networking time). Rules on absences and substitutes vary by group.

Some groups may also host "open house" type events to attract visitors who are potential members. Visiting a leads group is typically allowed only a couple of times before the group will ask the visitor to apply for membership or discontinue attending.

Pros of Leads Groups

Exclusivity. As mentioned earlier, this is one of the primary benefits a leads group can offer to members. The absence of direct competitors can draw favorable attention (and referrals!) to the one member holding that profession's slot in the group.

Friendship and Relationship Building. Business friendships can be fostered through continuous and frequent contact at meetings. Leads groups also encourage 1:1 (one-to-one) personal meetings between members outside of the regular meeting format to further strengthen these relationships.

Structure. Unlike looser networking venues where sales and connection opportunities can be haphazard, leads groups provide structure in terms of a standard meeting agenda, group organization, leadership positions and referral sharing procedures.

Leadership Opportunities. Opportunities to demonstrate and develop leadership skills are typically available to members, whether it be through volunteering to lead segments of the meeting agenda or taking on an executive/management role.

Focused Subgroups. Many leads groups have subgroups of allied professions which are designed to foster natural and logical referral sharing. For example, a healthcare subgroup may include a dentist, chiropractor, massage therapist and fitness trainer. These members may have similar types of clients which can be referred to other subgroup members.

Vetting Process. Membership is not guaranteed and member applicants must go through an approval process prior to joining. The vetting process and usually significant membership costs can help weed out those candidates who are not serious networkers.

Emphasis on Qualified Leads and Accountability. Some leads groups distinguish between "leads" and "referrals," with "leads" being less qualified and "referrals" representing genuine sales opportunities. Some groups will even discipline members who do not bring qualified or enough business opportunities to fellow members. This helps keep members accountable to the group.

Cons of Leads Groups

High Dollar Cost. Adding up the annual membership fee, meal fees, costs to do 1:1 meetings with members, travel and more, the financial investment in leads groups can be very high.

Exclusivity Games. In a desperate attempt to raise the number of members, some leads groups play games with exclusivity policies. For example, the "personal insurance" category might be broken down into three categories for life, auto and home. In the real world, though, people usually buy all three from one agent. Another example would be a health and beauty company where one representative says she'll represent skin care and the other says she'll promote makeup. This gaming of the system can actually can increase competition and infighting in the group.

Stagnation. Because memberships are for an entire year, and many members may choose to renew, the group can become stagnant due to it being comprised of the same individuals year, after year, after year. If the group has an active referral stream among members, this may not be a problem. But what can happen is that the group becomes a friendly clique with no other objective for meetings than to hang out with friends.

Referrals to Outside Sources. Members who are active in the business community may already have a strong network of sources outside the group for every imaginable service or product. So even if they do run across a lead for a fellow group member, they may be inclined to send it to their trusted outside source instead of the fellow member. This may not be done to intentionally hurt the other member; it's just that the outside source may be a better fit for the sales opportunity. That being said, it still can create dissent and disappointment which hurts everyone.

Internet Competition. Who needs a leads group when you have the Internet? Indeed, the Internet has had a negative impact on leads groups because anyone's next perfect vendor is only one click away.

Junk Leads. Finding leads and referrals for other people can be tough, really tough! So to save face in the group meetings, members may pass unqualified junk leads that never materialize.

Personal, Pity and "One and Done" Sales. Many members hope that there's at least one cheap product or service offered by a fellow member so that they can give a referral for their own personal purchase to meet their referral quota. For example, a nutritional supplement seller member may get a bunch of personal sales from fellow members seeking to meet their referral quotas. As well, some may feel badly for other members and make a personal purchase out of pity. These are often "one and done" purchases, too, since there really was no need for the product or service in the first place. Sadly, these can give a false sense that business is being shared when, in reality, the group is made up of ineffective members.

MLM Limitations. People who are representatives for multi-level marketing (MLM) organizations may be prohibited from soliciting their business opportunity in the group; some representatives may be banned entirely. Those groups that do allow MLM reps may restrict them to soliciting retail sales of their product or service only.

2 Key Factors to Consider

When considering a particular leads group or chapter, here are two key factors to consider when deciding whether it's worth the investment:

1. *Member Professions. Are enough professions represented in the group that are logical referral partners for your business? Is there a healthy mix of professions in the group or are there concentrations of artificially contrived subgroups?*

2. *Size of Group. How many members are in the group? If the group is small, that may indicate a newly established group with opportunity. But if it's been around for a number of years, and is still small or has trouble attracting members, it could be an indicator of problems such as those discussed in "Cons" above.*

CHAPTER 4:
What NOT to Do at Networking Events

There are some unwritten rules that new (even experienced!) networkers may violate without even realizing it. Are you guilty of any of these at networking events?

Don't Sit Down (at least not right away)!

You'll see them in almost any networking venue. Let's call them the "sitters." They arrive at the event and promptly plop their behinds in seats. Barring any physical ailment which might make standing impossible, why do networkers do this?

- **They're Special.** They could be a bit narcissistic. They act like networking is some kind of restaurant where the servers will bring food and new business connections right to their chairs.
- **They're Scared.** Actually, this is a more likely cause for the sitting behavior. They're either not prepared or lack confidence and the possibly of approaching people and striking up conversations is just too overwhelming.
- **They Don't Know What to Do.** Some newbies who have never experienced networking are just

not sure what's supposed to happen and how they fit into the whole affair.

There are portions of the meeting where sitting will be required and appropriate. Usually, these times will be announced. So until that signal is made, it's on your feet! **What to Do:** Stand up for your business!

Don't Be Incognito

This is a problem for both newbie networkers and highly experienced. Newbies may not know they need to wear a name badge so that people can put a face with a name. The old pros at it think everyone knows them so they don't need to wear one. They forget that there may be new people attending for the first time.

This is why some leads groups have official name badges for members that must be worn at EVERY meeting. Some groups even discipline those who habitually forget to bring and wear their badges!

What to Do: Get a professionally printed plastic or metal name badge for yourself and wear it at EVERY networking event or meeting. If the group has an official badge that members must wear, use that one instead and, if allowed, you could wear your own in addition. Your own badge that YOU buy will be part of your branding package. **TIP:** Wear your badge on your right side. Why? Because when people shake your right hand, their eyes will follow your right arm and shoulder up to your face. They'll be able to put YOUR name with YOUR face.

Don't be a Chatterbox

"Just shut up already!" That thought is often running through my head when someone I'm talking to drones on and on and on about Lord knows what. I don't want to be rude, but I'm going to look for any reason to extract myself from this person... stat!

What to Do: You want to get as many quality conversations into your networking experiences as possible. Circulate throughout the group! (Easier to do when you're standing on your feet instead of sitting, right? See first point on sitting above.) Reserve the long, in-depth conversations for 1:1 (one-to-one) personal meetings or phone call appointments outside the larger meetings and events.

Before an event, review what you might want to talk about that could be of interest to the other attendees... not just you. That will help keep you focused instead of blathering on and on.

Don't be a Know It All

I love it when someone I just met for 60 seconds has the answer or an opinion (usually negative) on everything.

What to Do: If you do have some insight to share with a networking connection, see if they'd be open to having a conversation with you outside the event or meeting. Don't be offended if they're not. Trust takes time.

Don't be a "Bragasaurus"

Okay, I know that might not be an official term for someone who feels compelled to talk only about himself. But like the dinosaurs this person is named after, he should be extinct in a networking environment.

What to Do: By all means be prepared to talk about your business and how you help people. But being a braggart alienates potential clients and friends. Check your ego at the door.

Don't Forget to Prep Your "Elevator Pitch"

Most networking events or groups have some sort of activity where you will be asked to tell everyone about you and your business in a very limited period of time, usually 30, 45 or 60 seconds. You may be thinking that's either a long time... or not enough.

To put this in perspective, try being silent for 30 and 60 seconds at a time. It will seem like an eternity! Now try to pack your story in that timeframe. That eternity turns into the blink of an eye.

What to Do: From the days when I was writing radio commercials, my personal rule of thumb was to keep a 15-second commercial to around 25 to 30 words. Actually, people can talk MUCH faster than that. But limiting it gives enough time to emphasize words and enunciate without getting out of breath.

This requires practice! Write it out. Say it in front of a mirror. Record yourself on a voice memo or recording device and play it back. Yes, play it back! It'll be difficult to listen to yourself at first. But remember that this is what your networking audience is hearing. Make it something they'll want to hear... especially emphasizing how you can serve THEM!

(We'll talk about how to write your elevator pitch in the following chapter.)

CHAPTER 5:
How to Write Your "Elevator Pitch" (aka "Your Networking Commercial")

What is an Elevator Pitch?

The term *elevator pitch* (sometimes referred to as an *elevator speech, networking commercial* or, in the business vernacular, a *"60-Second"*) is a very brief sales presentation that tells the seller's story in the time it takes for an elevator ride. Depending on the height of the building and how many stops the car makes, that time could be a few seconds up to a couple minutes. Having this pitch ready can help solopreneurs and consultants be prepared for chance encounters with prospects that may occur in an elevator (or anywhere!) at any time.

Networking events usually are not held in an elevator, of course. But the elevator pitch concept to create a networking "commercial" has become a standard used for face-to-face networking events since 30 to 60 seconds might be about all the time you have to connect with a potential prospect.

How to Write an Elevator Pitch

While there is no hard and fast formula and there can be myriad variations, an effective elevator pitch will usually be composed of these elements:

- *Your name, company (optional, but recommended) and what you do (for example, coach, marketing consultant, etc.).*
- *Who you help.*
- *How you help.*
- *Call to action.*
- *Your name, company and title again (although you may wish to just say your name), along with a memorable tagline (optional) at the end.*

It really is that simple! But I can't tell you how many elevator pitch fails I've heard over the years where people even forget to say their names!

Note that some networking groups, especially leads groups, may have a specific pitch formula they would like you to use. Use whatever is acceptable for the group.

"So an Elevator Pitch Needs to be 30 to 60 Seconds. How Many Words is That?"

I've taken my estimates on the number of words needed for a pitch from when I had to write some radio commercials. My rule of thumb was 25 to 30 words for each 15 seconds. Can you talk much faster than that? You sure can! But when you want people to really hear what you're saying, you need to slow it down, emphasizing each word and not sounding like you're running out of breath (and time!).

Prepare versions of your standard elevator pitch so that you're ready to deliver your message no matter what limited time you will be allowed. On the shortest pitch time (usually around 15 seconds), you may only be able to get in your name and a couple of words about what you do. But be ready for that!

Here's a handy reference:

- *60 seconds: 100 to 120 words*
- *30 seconds: 50 to 60 words*
- *15 seconds: 25 to 30 words*

How and When Should You Deliver Your Elevator Pitch?

In many networking groups and events, there will be a designated activity where attendees are given the opportunity to deliver their elevator pitch either to the entire group or to those people seated immediately around them.

Outside one of these formal activities, you would logically and naturally launch into your pitch when someone new asks what you do. Since you may already have shared your name when you introduce yourself to someone new, you would likely abbreviate your pitch to just include the "what you do" and "who you help" segments. In these cases, you might wind up and extend the conversation with something similar to one of the following, depending on your situation:

Option #1:

"Have you ever used a service (or product) like this and what was your experience?"

This option would be used if the person you are talking is an ideal candidate. You'd be surprised at what you might hear. Note that after you hear the answer, you shouldn't launch into a full blown sales pitch! But you would want to invite ideal prospects for a more in-depth conversation outside the event.

Option #2:
"Is there someone in your network who might be in need of what I have to offer?"

This second option honors the person's network and will encourage him to mentally scan his contacts for a possibility. If the person does have a connection for you, ask for an official introduction, possibly via email or social media. Do NOT contact any potential prospect until it is confirmed that the other person wants to hear from you.

These questions can make these folks dig a little deeper and, we hope, spend a bit more quality time with you.

CHAPTER 6:
Basic Business Card Tips

Business cards are one of the cheapest, easiest and most effective marketing tools. They're like little billboards and brochures. Here are some business card tips for using them effectively in sales and networking...

Not Ready to Work at Networking

At networking events, I usually meet up with some folks I might want to connect with afterward. So I typically ask them for a business card when I give them one of mine. Here are some responses I occasionally get:

- *"I don't have any on me."*
- *"I'm waiting for new cards."*
- *"Here, let me put my information on my boss' card [or some other non-related card they dig—and I do mean "dig"—out of a purse, wallet or pocket]."*

What? These people are going to an event designed for networking and don't have any business cards on them? Are they not planning on making any contacts for sales or other opportunities?

Okay, I'll cut these folks a bit of slack since many chamber of commerce and networking group events are primarily attended by familiar faces. So they may not be expecting to meet anyone new. But in my experience, there are usually a few new folks at every event. So I almost always carry about 20 to 50 business cards on me.

Business Card Tips for Networking:

Bring Enough. Always carry a supply of business cards wherever you go, especially to networking events! Depending on the event and its activities, that supply could be 20, 50 or more.

Wear or Carry Something with Pockets. A networking event is a performance art! Have a supply of business cards easily accessible to quickly and smoothly draw out a card to give. Keeping them ready in a jacket, slacks, skirt, or bag pocket makes it easy. Might even want to practice to make it a natural movement. No digging around in a bag or wallet!

Standard Business Card Size and Why to Use It

In case you're curious about what the standard business card size is, it is 3-1/2 inches wide by 2 inches high for horizontal or landscape orientation. For vertical or portrait orientation, it is 2 inches wide by 3-1/2 inches high.

In marketing, using odd size marketing materials can gain attention. But when it comes to business cards, stick with the standard size. Why? Though today people often enter the info from business cards electronically and then pitch the actual card, there are many who do still retain cards as backups. (Confession: I still use my business card files all the time!) Non-standard cards don't fit in any standard size storage containers or folders.

Here's an example of what happens when an odd size card is used.

A graphic designer I met once wanted to show how cool and creative she was. So, if I remember right, her business card was around 5 to 6 inches wide by 2-1/2 inches high. It was beautiful. However, I didn't know what to do with it. It didn't fit in any business card file I have. So I folded the darn thing to try to make it fit. It didn't. So then I resorted to trying to cut the card to fit. Let's see, should I cut off her business name or her contact info? After a few minutes of deciding what to do with it—and deciding that I wouldn't be needing services from her anytime soon—I put it in a container in which it would fit: the recycle bin.

Business Card Tips for Printing:

Use Standard Business Card Size. Fit your information within the 3-1/2 inches by 2 inches standard size limit (horizontal or vertical). It will cost less since special size cuts and papers can get expensive. As well, people will be more apt to file it away instead of throw it away. Use the size limitation to get creative.

Go Matte or Flat. Make sure that at least one side of the card does NOT include gloss or varnish coating to allow for people to write notes on it while networking.

Get Real. While it's tempting to print cards at home, they always look like they were printed at home. Many business cards available online are so cheap with good quality that it doesn't even pay to print them at home, especially when the cost of the special printer papers and ink cartridges is factored in.

Color Your World. Because full color printing is getting so cheap, there is little reason to stick with vanilla black-and-white business cards. Plus, it builds your brand.

Use Magnetic Business Cards Only Where Relevant. Only use magnetic business cards if the type of business demands it (home, on-demand or frequently used services could be candidates for them). With less magnetic surfaces available in homes and offices, they are less useful than in the past.

Why I Don't Put My Phone Number on My Business Cards, But Why You Might Want To

I don't put my phone number on my business cards. Shocked that someone in sales and networking would do that? I have my reasons. And, yes, they do deal with how I sell.

Years ago when I was doing some heavy networking, I put my phone number on my business cards and handed them out in stacks. It got me lots of phone calls, but not the ones I wanted.

Every person who wanted to sell to me decided that cold calling me on the phone was a good idea. Plus, there were the brain pickers and crackpots. They would phone me asking for marketing advice (for free, of course). Then there were those who wanted me to play therapist (again for free) on every imaginable business problem. Or they just wanted to rant about this topic or that.

It all amounted to a huge waste of my time. And since much of my work requires a significant amount of focus and concentration, I don't need calls from those who want my money, advice or attention without my consent. I cannot imagine ANY scenario where my writing or speaking services would require an emergency phone call for sales.

I handle phone calls the same way I handle in-person meetings which is by appointment. My sales funnel is designed to filter out those who absolutely cannot put into an email a few words about what their issues or needs are. That's a clear signal they don't know or understand what they're buying and could be problem clients.

HOWEVER... there are many businesses where a phone number is absolutely essential on a business card. Plumbing, heating, towing, ambulance, and urgent healthcare centers would be prime examples of those that need it included. Any business that provides emergency help or is set up to handle telephone sales would need a phone number on a card. For these folks, email might be the contact info they eliminate!

Business Card Tips for Contact Info:

Consider Your Sales Funnel. Do you want business to come to you by phone, email, Internet or by people wandering into a brick-and-mortar location? Let your sales funnel(s) guide what contact information elements should be included or given prominence on the card.

Not at Home. For home-based businesses that do not want people stopping by, including a physical address can present a host of annoyance, privacy and security issues. Use a post office box or eliminate the physical address entirely. Also consider using separate business phone lines for similar security and privacy reasons.

Why I Use My Photo on My Business Cards, But Why You Might NOT Want To

Because I'm a speaker and author, and I want people I meet to remember me, I use my photo on my business cards. This has been an amazing sales and networking tactic for me. When I attend subsequent events, people can usually remember who I am. Why? Because they can put a face with a name.

As well, it fosters a feeling of trust for customers who know there's a real person behind the name. That's why businesses such as real estate and insurance often use their photos on business cards.

But this tactic isn't for everyone. Those who feel that having their photo and contact info together out in public presents a security risk should not do it.

For those whose insecurity is more about being self-conscious and embarrassed, using a photo on the business card could cause them to refrain from handing out any cards, thereby reducing sales and opportunities.

Business Card Tips for Photos:

Let Emotional and Security Needs Guide Photo Decisions. If including a photo presents a safety or emotional security risk, don't use it!

Face It. If security issues are not a problem and the recognition factor is desired, using a headshot on a business card can be a great networking tool.

What About Electronic Business Cards?

Confession: A few years ago, I predicted the eventual demise of the standard paper business card. I was wrong. But why did I make that prediction?

About 2008 or so, social media and mobile technology were exploding. We were using social media to make connections even when in person. We were bumping mobile phones to exchange data. The era of seamless electronic data exchange seemed to be upon us. So why are we still exchanging little slips of paper?

Social media is a chaotic universe. It changes almost every day. Plus, there are so many networks and not everyone is on every one. Mobile tech is evolving faster than we can almost keep up. The ways that these devices communicate with one another changes frequently, too. And not everyone has the latest tech. Plus, if transfer of data requires Wi-Fi, the ability to connect will depend on the strength of the signals. So making connections electronically while in person is still a challenge.

Business Card Tips for Today's Networking:

Go New School AND Old School. Stay mindful of and experiment with new tech and trends for exchanging information, but ALWAYS have business cards ready to make a connection no matter what!

CHAPTER 7:
Do Your Business Cards Scream
"I'm a Newbie!" or "I'm Not a Pro!"?

In the last chapter, we talked about what your business card should be in terms of printing and handling. Here we'll talk about what your card says, not only in terms of actual words, but the subliminal messages you might be unintentionally sending with your design and distribution procedures.

The 11 Deadly Business Card Sins

Do your business cards—whatever you're using now as you begin your new or renewed business networking adventures—have any of these qualities?

1. *Old email address, especially one that uses a free email service or ISP such as AOL (one of the oldest), Yahoo or Gmail.*
2. *No website.*
3. *Job title that says something like "coach" or "consultant" without specifying what type of coaching or consulting you do.*
4. *Vanity title such as President or CEO of your solopreneur micro business.*

5. *Back of the business card says something such as "Get your own FREE business cards from Such-and-Such Budget Online Printer."*
6. *Dug up from the bowels of your bag or pocket.*
7. *Everyone has your card.*
8. *A card from a different or previous business, handed out while saying, "I only have these cards from my other XYZ business."*
9. *Includes every imaginable social media link.*
10. *Using brochures instead of business cards.*
11. *No business cards at all.*

The problem really isn't the business cards themselves. Each of these items is a symptom of a much greater problem with a business. Let's break 'em down...

1. Old Email Address

You might have had a fancy-schmancy prestigious email address before you left a corporate job. And, of course, you cannot use your old corporate email address anymore. But getting a branded email (along with website domain, as we'll discuss in a moment) is a pretty cheap affair these days. Get one! Otherwise, people might think you're either in career transition or hurting for money if you use a free email service.

2. No Website

Getting a domain name and website is so easy and cheap these days, that to not have either can send signals that you are cheap, too.

Getting your own name is a popular domain name choice (if you feel comfortable with that) especially for those who are personally doing consulting and coaching.

Potential clients will likely search online (usually on Google) for your name and having a domain name and website that is your name can assist in finding you more quickly. Be aware that domain registrars offer what's called "private registration" service for an added fee that helps protect your personal information. See your registrar's website for options and pricing.

If your own name is not available or you don't want to use it, use your company's name or a tagline. Even with these domains, private registration is typically available.

Many domain providers also offer a basic website with the purchase of a domain name registration, as well as an email address with the domain name. That site won't likely be your permanent web home, but it will suffice until you're more established. And having your own branded email in the meantime is a huge plus.

If even setting up that most basic domain package website is daunting, forward the domain to one of your complete and current online profiles. This can serve as a web presence until you're able to invest in something more elaborate.

3. The Mystery Coach or Consultant

This isn't the worst sin of the lot. But it can seriously affect how people, especially potential clients, remember you (or don't!). Always include a statement or more descriptive title that clearly conveys what you do and how you help.

Two of the most problematic fields are "life coaching" and "business coaching." Within those two arenas are probably hundreds of types of work that can be done. If your field falls within an over-general category like this, make sure that your card includes some sort of statement about your specialty, the kind of people you help or the problems you help solve.

More mystery titles and descriptions include:

XYZ or Some Obscure Term followed by "Associates," "Enterprises" or "Group." Um, what does your company do? And, if you're a solo business, who are those "associates" and "group" members?

Job Title of (Insert Buzzword Here)-ologist or Chief (Insert Buzzword Here) Officer. Again, what do you do?

"Specializing in Success" or "Solutions for Success" or Other Non-Specific Tagline. Success defined as... ? Who and how do you help?

4. Vanity Title

On your business registration you might have stated that your official title is "president" or "CEO." But putting that on your business card for your micro business can be quite amusing. You're not fooling anyone. No one will mentally put you on par with the likes of CEO-types such as Bill Gates. Better to go with a "coach" or "consultant" type title related to the work you do.

5. Free Business Cards

These days, business cards are cheap. Like really cheap. I remember back in the day when some super vanilla thermographic printed black-and-white business cards could run into the hundreds of dollars for a small batch. Not today! Today, we can get beautiful, professional, full color business cards, printed on both sides for very little money. So why would you consider getting those freebie business cards that are given to you free because you agree to host the printer's advertising on the back? No, they're not doing you any favors.

You don't have to get all the extra services such as gloss coating, metallic inks and the like. In fact, you don't actually want glossy cards. Try writing a note on one of those babies. A ballpoint pen won't even work. And if you use those roller ball type pens, you'll hand your prospects smeared cards that could leave ink on their hands, maybe even their clothing. Is that how you want to be remembered?

6. Diggin' In

I would just love to shoot some video of those folks who are just not prepared for the networking experience. What would I be shooting? Video of them digging through their purses, pockets or bags for a business card at an event. It's actually quite hilarious. *"I know I have one somewhere."* Or, to appear that they've been so busy networking, *"I hope I didn't run out of cards."* Then when they finally produce said card, it's usually bent or worn at the corners. Yeah, I really want to do business with someone who isn't ready for business.

Sometimes when you order business cards, they'll include a flimsy, but serviceable, free business card holder. If you can't afford a better quality business card holder, use that until you can. But use some type of holder to protect your precious networking tools. Then keep your business card holder at the ready in a clothing pocket or easily accessible area of your bag.

And while you're building your networking toolkit, get a professional name badge with your name at minimum. Adding your company name or a few words about what you do to the badge is optional, but recommended. Remember to wear your badge on the right chest so that when you extend your hand to shake that of your next client prospect, he'll see your name and put it with your face, regardless of whether he eventually gets your business card or not.

7. Everyone Has Your Card

Are you pushing your cards onto everyone you meet at a networking event? Please, stop! This is a sign of an insecure businessperson who thinks no one will want his or her card (which, sadly, might be correct). And I'll let you in on a dirty little secret. Even if your unwilling card recipients appear glad to get your cards, they'll throw them out as soon as they get back to the office.

Wait until the conversation has advanced to the point where a future connection is discussed. Then ask for a business card exchange... and when you should follow up.

8. Ghosts of Jobs Past and Shadow Careers

You're so new that you don't even have your business cards yet. But you're anxious to start networking so you figure, *"Heck, I'll just use my old business cards, cross out my old info and write in the new stuff."* The message you're giving off? *"I'm a noob!"* If someone is coming to you with a life or business problem, do you think he or she will want to be your new business' guinea pig?

Would you want to be a surgeon's first patient? I think I've made my point.

Then there are those who are still running another business and/or plan to continue to do so. No problem there. Lots of people do have multiple streams of income, either to fund a new operation or because it's a good operational fit for the future. But the problem is that if you hand out these "shadow" business cards while you're talking up your new business, people might associate you with the old or other business and wonder if you're really committed to this new venture.

9. Includes Every Imaginable Social Media Link

Okay, I'll admit it. Back around 2010 or so, I was including every social media link on my business cards. Heck, it was being heralded as THE new way to do marketing. Fast forward to now. Social media is used by almost everyone and the various social networks are in a constant state of flux. Yesterday's social media "It" network could be today's has-been.

Of course, if your business revolves around this or that social network, then include that one on your card. Otherwise, you can just include all your current and relevant (meaning relevant for your business) social media links on your website instead of loading up valuable real estate on your business card. With social media being as prevalent as it is today, people will probably assume you're on social media regardless of whether you include links on your business card or not.

10. Using Brochures Instead of Business Cards

Then there are the "brochures posing as business cards." Here's what's happening:

Too Cheap to Buy Both Business Cards AND Brochures. Folks, business cards are cheap these days. If given the choice, get your cards first, then invest in brochures. Brochures can be a major investment, especially if you're just starting out. Focus on business cards and your website first since they can be much more effective, versatile and portable marketing tools.

Tell All, Sell Nothing. Small business people often are praying that potential customers will be sooooooo impressed with EVERYTHING the company does, that they're bound to buy something. This "see what sticks" strategy is usually not a winning one. Those who substitute using their full brochures for business cards could have fallen into this sales trap.

What your card (oops, brochure) says: *"I'm cheap and am keeping my fingers crossed that I'll make some kind of sale... any sale (PLEASE!)."*

11. No Business Cards at All

I've saved the worst for last. There's nothing more damaging to a new business than telling a potential prospect you just met, *"I don't have any business cards."* This says:

- *"I don't believe in my business... yet (or at all). So I'm not going to spend a dime."*
- *"I don't know what I'm doing... yet (or at all)."*
- *"I'm afraid to promote my business... just in case it doesn't work out."*

Regardless of how tech savvy we've gotten, your business card is your primary in-person networking tool. Have your tools ready before you do your network "work."

CHAPTER 8:
Why You Don't Need to Be on Every Social Media Network

The same show or sporting event doesn't broadcast on every network. So why should you when it comes to social media? Yet, small businesses scramble and struggle to keep up with every available social media network.

In our discussion here about networking with social media, I'm not even going to go through the pros and cons of every network. Or even how to use them. Why? Because by the time this publishes, those networks will likely have changed, rendering my tips obsolete. Plus, "hot" new networks are constantly springing up and going down.

What we will discuss are the strategies behind using social media, regardless of network.

Some Businesses May be Prohibited, Restricted or Regulated in the Use of Social Networking

Finance, investments, law and healthcare are just a few of the businesses for whom social networking is professionally prohibited, restricted or regulated. But other industries may also have serious restrictions, too. Consult the governing authorities for your industry or profession and seek legal advice for guidelines as to what is permissible or prohibited in terms of networking on social media for you.

Being "On" Social Media Doesn't Necessarily Mean Being "Actively On"

Ever visit a website and the entire top navigation bar is loaded with every social media icon available? Then when each one is clicked it goes to an account where no one is home.

Merely having an account on the various social networks does not necessarily mean being "actively on" that network.

Being active on a social media network means that the business is regularly posting content or status updates and having interaction with other users on that network. **Those social media channels where a business is truly active should be the only ones promoted.** Nothing says *"we don't care"* or *"we don't know what the heck we're doing"* more than a dead blog or social media account.

Reserving accounts on the major social platforms in a company's name is definitely recommended to protect the business' brand name. However, for social media networks where the accounts are simply placeholders, redirect visitors to the main website or other truly active social media accounts.

"Like Us On Facebook?"

I almost have to laugh as I drive down the road and whiz by a variety of business vehicles that have big signs on them that say *"Like Us on Facebook."* I wonder if these folks, as well meaning as they might be, really expect that to happen. I also wonder what results they hope to achieve, though I do have to applaud them for making the effort to keep their marketing relevant and current.

Let's take on-demand type businesses such as for health, emergency home care, transportation services or pizza (all of which I have seen promote their social media accounts on vehicles). If potential customers are faced with an immediate need, they are not likely to wander over to a social network to do some searching. These frantic customers are much more likely to go to Internet search than social media.

As discussed earlier, businesses should definitely protect their branding with reserving social media accounts in the business' name and brand names. They may even wish to populate the account with some helpful posts and resource links. However, other marketing tools may have a bigger impact and be worthy of consideration. For example, with more and more smartphones in the population, access to the Internet anytime anywhere is becoming more and more common, making mobile websites and mobile search Internet advertising campaigns viable options to consider.

Bottom line is that not every social media network is right for every business. Choosing the right one will depend on the following factors:

- *Business goals for being on any of the social networks.*
- *Personality and preferences of both the business and the market served.*

47

- *Time and resources available to post and be actively on the network.*

CHAPTER 9:
5 Mistakes Networkers Make with Social Media Profiles

Your social media profiles are like your social media business cards! There are five primary profile mistakes that I've seen businesspeople make when using social media for networking:

*1. **Irrelevant Photos.*** As suggested for printed business cards which use photos, use a good headshot of YOU. Though what you can use in terms of shape and size will depend on the network you're using, crop it to primarily feature your face. Some people try to use full body shots which are completely unidentifiable when viewed in the reduced pixel display area for the profile photo. Worse yet are those users who use pictures of their kids, pets, favorite possessions, cars... it's just ridiculous. We don't want to follow your kid or cat, no matter how adorable. We want to follow YOU! The only exception is for an official company account (such as a business page) that could include the company's logo in this spot.

*2. **No Location or Goofy Location.*** Early in the days of social media, some users thought it was cool to use their longitude and latitude locations. Guess what? Most people won't go through the steps to interpret where that really is. Others wanted to be cute and enter locations such as *"Everywhere," "Earth"* or *"Cyberspace."* No, we're not asking you to enter your home address (never, ever!), but people often want to know if they're connecting with those in their own country, metropolitan area, state or region. Use something easily identifiable, but generic enough to help maintain your security and privacy.

3. Generic Bios. If I had a dime for every social media profile that included useless, generic phrases to define how the user is special, I'd be able to retire without even finishing writing this book. Some truly awful examples: *"I'm a husband/wife/father/mother/friend," "I love to meet people,"* or *"Enjoying life."* Those would describe the majority of people on this planet. How are you different? What can we expect you to be posting about? Even worse are the ones who don't fill in the bio at all. I don't follow anyone who doesn't fill in a bio. Period.

4. Buzzword Bios. Please, make it stop! I seriously don't want to see another profile with *"creative," "innovative," "results-oriented," "passionate"*… and similar buzzwords. Just search Google for buzzwords in LinkedIn profiles and you'll see what I'm talking about. If you're *"results-oriented,"* what results do you offer? That's what we want to see in your profile.

5. No Website Link. As discussed earlier for print business cards, not having a website can say a lot about your business. An investment worth considering.

CHAPTER 10:
Why "Know, Like and Trust" is NOT Enough

One of the reasons marketers have gravitated toward social networking is that it can help build long-term rapport with potential customers in a non-sales, non-threatening way. (Not to mention the fact that getting a presence on the social networks is usually "free"... well, in terms of hard dollars at least.) The goal is that when followers need the product or service offered, the marketer has top of mind awareness. Prospects and customers come to know, like and trust the marketer, creating warm sales leads. That is the true purpose of networking with social media and it has done very well for me.

But here's the problem: "know, like and trust" doesn't automatically lead to sales leads.

No Need, No Sales, No Problem?

I am so honored to have thousands of followers on Twitter, as well as hundreds of followers and readers in my immediate area and around the world. Many of them know, like and trust me enough to the point where we've been able to establish relationships offline in real life.

Many have also become clients, dear friends and mutually beneficial resources.

But I've realized that most of my followers, online and off, will never, ever buy my standard product and service offerings. Primarily, this is because they often don't have the need or authority to buy, even if they're interested in the topics I discuss. They may not even have friends they can refer to me. Some are even friendly competitors.

And that's okay... really it is.

I'm very, VERY appreciative of the support and friendship my followers provide. Many have changed my life forever.

But when it comes to using social media for business, I definitely have some sales objectives. And I'm very mindful of the difference between the friendship and financial paths these efforts can take.

So how do I separate the two paths and prevent myself from mistaking friendship as productivity? Trust me, it's not easy.

The Social Media Black Hole

Some years back, social media was really turning the marketing arena upside down. And I wanted to make a name for myself in that emerging space. To some extent I did. But what did it cost?

Starting back around 2009, I was spending a large amount of time on the social networks, somewhere on the order of three to four hours a day, even on the weekends. Blogging a blue streak, too, which took additional hours.

I was gaining new followers and was having a LOT of communication.

Finally, in late 2010, I was getting exasperated and exhausted. (The recession didn't help either.) Luckily, I was smart enough to recognize that my small business needed some outside professional help. I told my new business strategy coach about my social media exploits and achievements and how I felt pretty proud of my thousands of fans and such. Know what his response was?

"So what?"

"So what?" Really? Didn't he know how hard I worked to achieve this? Basically, my coach pointed out how I really had little to show for spending nearly half a standard workday every day on the social networks. But here's why this is a problem:

Communication does NOT equal Conversion!

Have I ditched social media as a result? Of course not! It's still bringing traffic and opportunities my way, though I'm no longer falling into a rabbit hole of low productivity and high stress. But it does take a strategy.

Managing And Monitoring Social Networking For Business

One of the first things my coach emphasized is that a business needs to be run by the numbers. Not just any numbers. The right numbers. Those right numbers include such things as profit margins, website traffic and conversion rates, but NOT follower counts on social media networks. So I did a thorough analysis of my website traffic. What an enlightening exercise!

I found that very little of my blog traffic was being generated by social media, except for traffic from Twitter. Then traffic from my blog to one of my shopsites was significant. But the problem was that this particular shopsite was not the one generating sales leads. What did this mean? Well, possibly a lot of tire kickers or those simply curious, not serious, were coming from the blog.

The biggest traffic driver on most of my shopsites was coming from organic search (SEO). That's good. But it also meant that my social media frenzy might not be driving sales. When I ask new customers how they found me, they usually respond "through search." Case closed for me.

However, in my F2F (face-to-face) networking, I have encountered a number of people who have made significant sales from social media networks. Often these are in the B2C (business-to-consumer) category. Use whatever works for you!

Here are some things that I've done to manage and monitor my business' social media presence:

Monitor Social Media Traffic to Web Properties. Set up Google Analytics (or other web traffic monitoring system) for each website owned. Don't guess how much traffic is being generated by social media. Know! Today I usually watch traffic numbers to all my sites monthly at minimum, with more detailed analysis quarterly and annually. Monitoring frequency necessary will be determined by the nature of the website and business being promoted.

Don't Worry About Follower Counts. While certainly one needs to encourage people to join a business' "tribe" on social networks, obsessing over follower counts is counterproductive.

Limit, Schedule and Organize Time on Social Media. Set a time limit that will be spent on social media and schedule when that time will be. For example, I set 30 minutes aside on weekday mornings (no weekends!) to check and post to primary social media feeds. Consider it a standing sales call. Using a social media management system such as HootSuite.com can assist in pre-scheduling posts and tweets, as well as organizing incoming feeds to save time on reading.

Know What You're "Selling." In some cases, non-sales traffic can still be profitable. For example, if a blog or other site generates advertising revenue, then driving traffic to it from social media is a good thing, regardless of whether the visitors actually buy the company's traditional offerings or not. But know that what's being "sold" is advertising, not invitations to buy products and services.

Realize "What Happens on Social Media Stays on Social Media." One of the counterproductive aspects of social media for business can be the tendency for conversations to remain on the network and never move to a company's website. For entertainment or casual friendships that might be fine. But if the goal is to transact and attract business, this results in a social media black hole. This is where measuring traffic from social networks to the company's websites and then comparing to the levels of activity and investment can be helpful.

Understand the Social Networking Time Cost. While setting up accounts on social media networks is typically free, the cost in terms of time and effort can be HUGE. Try this exercise. Multiply the hourly rate you earn by the amount of time you spend on social media per day. Go ahead try it. Small business owners and entrepreneurs would prorate their annual revenue to get an hourly cost. Even if you earned only $10 an hour, spending 30 minutes a day only on weekdays would cost you $1,300 per year in labor. Shocked? And if employees are also doing this, imagine how much this can cost an organization!

CHAPTER 11:
Are You an Over-Networker?

There's one (often more) in every networking group: "The Over-Networker." She (I've seen more women in this mode than men) goes to almost EVERY possible event or meeting being held in the immediate area. At an event, she will pursue almost EVERY new person who walks into the room in an overly familiar manner that would make anyone want to find the nearest exit... fast!

The mental fallacy behind this behavior is that over-networkers believe the more events and meetings they attend, and the more people they can connect with, the more attention they will receive. Technically, they're correct. Other people will likely notice how omnipresent they are. They also falsely reason that with this exposure frequency, they will automatically become THE top-of-mind source for whatever it is they sell. Indeed, while they may become the top-of-mind source, they may not ultimately be the CHOSEN source. They may even become top-of-mind for the "People to Avoid Next Time" list.

Another false belief is also at work for them. Over-Networkers believe that ALL networking groups, connections and events are equally valuable. As discussed in the previous chapter on *"Types of Networking Groups,"* this is just not the case.

Instead of choosing what groups and events are most advantageous for them, over-networkers take a "panning for gold" approach and chase every vein of sales and networking gold, no matter how small.

What a waste... usually with little to show for it!

Busy-ness or Business?

One of the other qualities of over-networkers is that they are so busy running from one networking event to the next, sometimes attending multiple events in the same day, that they rarely stop to figure out whether their over-networking is producing anything. It's also not uncommon for over-networkers to sacrifice valuable family and personal time in the name of networking, too.

The Friendship Fallacy

Another belief fueling the over-networking trap is "friends do business with friends." True, if given the choice, many people would rather do business with a less competent friend than a competent stranger.

But here's what happens. Over-networkers will attend a slew of events and meetings where they know they'll connect with friends, both those that could become clients and those that are not ready, willing and able to take that buying step. Because it's so nice to meet with friends, they can justify the spending of time or money, regardless of the results.

Don't be fooled into thinking this only happens in F2F (face to face) real life events. People can easily be lulled into thinking they're really doing business when they over-share and over-engage online. Whether it's being on the social networks for hours a day, sharing too much information or being super active on too many networks. What's even more amusing is that some of these online over-networkers then brand themselves as social media "gurus" even if they haven't made a dime. *"Show me the money!"*

Preventing Over-Networking

Here are some fundamental prevention steps to keep you from becoming an over-networker:

- *Evaluate Networking Groups and Events in Advance.* Take a look at the people who will be attending. Don't just look for specific people you know. Look at the work the members or attendees do and the organizations they represent. Are they a good fit for your organization? If not, it's *"Next!"*

- *Evaluate the Opportunity Cost.* Don't equate activity with results. Measure! Every networking activity takes time, energy and expense away from something else in your business or personal life. Later on, we'll discuss how to measure your networking success.

Bottom line: Choose carefully, don't chase.

GIVING AND GETTING BUSINESS THROUGH NETWORKING

CHAPTER 12:
How to Give a Good Referral

Surprised we're starting this off with a discussion on "giving" referrals for sales? Well, many networking groups focus on giving to others BEFORE expecting to get. We'll follow that tradition and start with how to give.

What is a Referral?
Many networking groups and associations differentiate between "leads" and "referrals."

A *lead* is considered an unsubstantiated opportunity that merely points out potential for another. For example, someone notices that a new coffee shop is opening and he alerts a marketing consultant in his network of the new store. Typically, no personal introductions are made. The person who receives the lead often pursues it blindly. This is one step up from a cold call. As well, the person passing the lead may not even have permission to share any information with the salesperson. Later, we'll discuss why that's a problem, too.

A *referral* is considered a genuine, identified sales opportunity where someone knows of a current and real need of a friend, family member or colleague that could be handled by a networking partner. In these cases, the two parties are introduced to each other, identifying the need to be addressed. Consent to introduce is a key element of these introductions and is the first element in the following formula for more successful referrals.

The C.A.R.E. Formula for a Good Referral

Giving a referral is a sign that you care about the people you are referring to each other. But a referral must meet some criteria in order to be of value to everyone. So here is a quick formula to test a potential referral opportunity BEFORE you engage anyone.

Using C.A.R.E. as an acronym, here are the elements of a good referral:

"C" is for Consent. Before you blindly blast off an email or social media connection to two potential referral connections, get consent from both. For example, say that you know Referral Partner A would be an excellent supplier or resource for Referral Partner B. Before you email contact info to either partner, you'll want to ask both separately and privately if they are interested in connecting. If both agree, then a connection is warranted. Additionally, in today's era of concern over data privacy and sharing of personal information, this aspect of sharing referrals is critical and cannot be ignored!

You might be thinking, *"Why wouldn't Partner A be interested in connecting with Partner B as a potential customer?"* Seriously, I have received innumerable forced referrals over the years that were totally inappropriate potential clients for me. These junk referrals not only wasted my time, but had the potential to harm my reputation since I was seen as someone who was unable to serve the prospective Partner B customer's needs. As well, Partner B could peg the person who made the referral as someone who doesn't have a competent network and/or who can't professionally evaluate sales opportunities. Which brings us to the next element in the formula...

"A" is for Actual. Sometimes people want to impress either the person they're referring or the person who will receive the referral. So they connect colleagues in their network, regardless of whether an actual opportunity exists or not. Can these lead to sales at some point in the future? Sure, it's possible. But sometimes it's a long shot. If no immediate or imminent need exists, don't personally connect the parties.

"R" is for Relevant. Just as with actual need, a referral must be relevant for both parties. For example, I am a self publishing coach for business books. So inquiries for people who are looking for an author agent for fiction are not relevant to me, even though both I and the author agent work with authors on books. Make sure that you understand both the needs of your friends or colleagues and the source you are referring to them.

"E" is for Exit and Evaluate. Once you have properly introduced two parties, it's usually best for you to exit the transaction picture and let them explore the potential opportunity themselves. However, it doesn't hurt to follow up and evaluate whether the referral was a success, after a sufficient amount of time has passed for the type of business and people you are referring. You do want to know whether you should refer these people to others in the future. As well, you want to get an idea if

your referral radar is working properly. If it isn't, you'll want to get to know your network a whole lot better!

Checklist for a Good Referral

Here's a checklist of items that make up a good referral. **IMPORTANT: When contacting each party for the referral, do NOT reveal either party's name or info until you receive permission privately from each one.**

- *Name of person(s) being referred.*
- *Preferred method of contact for all parties (email, phone, social media, etc.).*
- *Contact info for preferred method.*
- *Best time to reach (if known).*
- *Exact product or service of interest and/or other reason for contact.*
- *Best way to schedule appointment (if known).*
- *Budget for purchase (if applicable and known).*

CHAPTER 13:
Getting Better Referrals for Your Business

Big Hug or Big Shrug?

This is tough! I'm so thankful that caring people in my network have thought well enough of me to refer me to their family or friends. But if who they're referring is a bad fit, my response will go from *"meh"* to *"What's the least painful way to deal with this, for both them and me?"*

It's not that I don't want referrals. I just don't want bad referrals that will only waste my time, as well as possibly ruin my reputation and that of the referring party.

Dealing with Bad Referrals

As non-committal as this sounds, how I deal with bad referrals I receive depends on several factors including:

The Person Referring. Is the person referring me someone whose feelings will be hurt badly when they realize that they've given a bad referral? I'll handle both the referring party and the person being referred with some TLC and diplomacy. Is this person still new to the networking arena and someone who doesn't have their opportunity identification skills honed yet? This could be a great teaching moment... again, delivered with a dose of TLC. Or is this person just trying to impress either me or the party being referred? I'll have to be very clear with that person about my needs and how I would like to handle the current and future referral situations.

The Person Being Referred. If the person being referred, even if not an ideal sales prospect, is someone I truly would like to connect with, I may make the connection, but be very clear that I may not be a good fit for the current need. I may also offer some suggestions for other suitable resources. That way both I and the person who referred me look like heroes.

You Might be the Reason Why You're Getting Bad Networking Referrals

This might be difficult to hear, but you may be causing those bad referrals. Yes, YOU!

I learned this lesson while I was transitioning my business to self publishing coaching from being in a couple different business lines for many years. Started out by telling people I was a *"marketing coach."* Am I? I sure am. I help speakers, coaches and consultants use self published books and blogs to build their brands. But when people heard *"marketing coach,"* they immediately associated me with those who do social media marketing, SEO consulting, direct mail, Internet advertising (such as Google AdWords)... and the list went on.

Adding to the problem was that I also was telling people that I worked with small businesses. Huge mistake! Are the businesses I work with small? You bet! Usually, they're solopreneurs or self-employed consultants. But as soon as I said *"small business,"* I started getting referrals from and for multi-level marketers and lots of local service businesses, none of which I can help in any substantial way.

So how did I beat the bad referrals? I had to be very specific about the kind of business and the kind of client I wanted. When I revamped my networking "story," I started getting more referrals and, more importantly, more relevant ones.

It starts with you.

Getting Your Referral Story Straight

To get people to respond and refer to you correctly, you've got to get your "story" straight by being clear about:

What You Do. Just as I wasn't giving people anything to go on when I said I do marketing, you can't be vague when you say how you help people. Be very clear about the exact products or services you offer and/or the results that you help people achieve.

Who You Help. Your networking partners need to be able to visualize someone that you could help. For example, saying that you work with women is so vague that people can think of too many possibilities and get overwhelmed... and overwhelm you with a lot of irrelevant referrals. Saying that you work with women who are over 40 and thinking about starting a different career would be easier for people to peg.

How You Would Like to be Contacted. This is important! For example, because I need to set aside around a half hour to talk to a potential client prospect, I do NOT want to be randomly contacted by phone. So I ask that my networking partners introduce me to potential clients via email first. Then both I and the referred party can schedule a mutually agreeable time to talk and be prepared to give proper attention to the conversation. On the other hand, your business may be very dependent on selling over the phone and/or be an on-demand service. Then giving out your phone number might be appropriate. Don't presume people will know how to refer you.

Your Business Card. Your business card should tell potential clients and referral partners ALL of the above.

Being in the Right Networks. Another important aspect of the referral process is being in the right networks that know or include the kinds of people you want to meet. This sounds so obvious. But it's amazing how many times I'll meet someone at a networking event and wonder why he or she is even there. Hey, I've wondered that about myself at some events, too. For example, many small business people join their local chamber of commerce. Logically, that's a great idea. But if the small business' clientele is nationwide or international, this may not be the best venue. It might take some trial and error visits to various groups (either in person or online groups) to discover those that work. Save time and effort by only participating in networking that puts you in touch with those who are relevant to you and your business.

CHAPTER 14:
What About Competitors at Networking?

Warning! You WILL encounter competitors, possibly many of them, when networking! I've even been to events where there were up to five sales representatives of the same product. Imagine that! Plus, if you attend networking events for your industry, you might be bumping into a whole room full of competitors.

Should you be cautious, or fearful, of competitors you'll encounter during networking? Of course, sharing of confidential information and trade secrets, price fixing and the like are strictly prohibited, even illegal, activities with competitors!

But realize that having representation at relevant networking events positions your business as one of many potential vendors. It also affords an opportunity to make friendly relationships with competitors for either partnering or referrals should the need arise.

Here's an example. In one of my networking groups, two competitors selling the exact same product from the exact same manufacturer partnered up for a charity fundraising project. Both businesses looked like professional colleagues concerned about the community. A win for both competitors and the manufacturer they represented.

I've also benefitted personally from maintaining friendly relationships with competitors. When I wanted to shut down one profit center of my business, I had to decide what to do with a portfolio of clients who had been loyal to me for many years. Luckily, I had established a number of friendly connections with competitors in the area and one of them was an ideal fit for this group of clients. I was so thankful that this competitor was in my network so that I had someone to take care of my customers while I took my business to the next level.

Remember competitors are as much a part of your community and network as customers. Always be positive and professional when dealing with them!

CHAPTER 15:
Why to Avoid the Disguised Sales Pitch

A call from a long time (or long lost) friend or colleague pops up on the voicemail or email. Wow! Great to hear from them, right? *"We need to catch up. Have time for a quick phone call?"* Why not?

The day and time arrives. The old friend is right on time. *"Hey, just wanted to see how you're doing."* The conversation moves from kids to kitchen remodeling to remembering that guy Kevin from accounting. Then it takes an abrupt turn. *"I'm now with XYZ company and I'm selling widgets..."* Here it comes: The Sales Pitch.

Really?

Here's what's happening. The old friend is rolling through his Rolodex and searching for old contacts for his new job, business, project or whatever. Needs to make the numbers with new gig! This is almost a bait-and-switch tactic. The friendly check-in which morphs into a sales call.

Unfortunately, the only thing the caller will gain from the encounter is a tick mark on the calls made checklist. But what he's lost is so much more: Trust and a friend. The friend will wonder if all future calls will be disguised sales calls. Very uncomfortable. Very unprofitable. It's almost worse than cold calling!

Discussed here will be motivations behind this behavior and some relationship preserving alternatives for connecting for business and sales purposes.

Feedback Foul

Getting feedback from relevant colleagues and friends outside the company is a great way to test ideas before making offerings publicly available. But some salespeople turn these valuable inputs into a disguised sales pitch. Here's how that goes...

"Hey, can I get your feedback on a new assessment tool I'm developing?" The unsuspecting contact agrees and takes the time to go through the entire process. The assessment with feedback is returned to the old colleague who then promptly sends back a proposal for getting hired. Yes, this is based on an actual reported incident! The prospect was irritated he had spent time reviewing the assessment and branded his old buddy as pushy.

Why did the person do this? It's likely that he realized it would be difficult to obtain a request for a proposal from his friend. So asking for "feedback" was much easier.

Qualification Quest

Another dig through the Rolodex may uncover potential prospects that a seller needs to qualify to decide whether to pitch or ditch this one. So why not schedule an "update" call?

The update call seems to be going nowhere. It's nice to catch up. But through some veiled or awkward questions, it appears the salesperson is putting together a profile of whether this one is a prospect possibility.

If the calls ends with, *"Well, it was great to chat. Take care. Bye."* No "next step" dialog. No *"Let's grab a coffee soon."* The friend's been ditched. If there's some glimmer of hope for a sale, then the pitch would likely have occurred immediately.

Sure, networkers need to qualify prospects. But burning through one's database of friendlies will burn some communication bridges, too.

Why Do We Disguise Sales Pitches?

There is one and only one reason for this selling and networking behavior: fear. We're afraid that there will be resistance if we come right out and disclose why we're calling or connecting. Also, when we become uneasy about approaching old or new contacts, we may resort to leaving mystery phone messages.

A bit of anxiety when approaching prospects— whether they're new or old contacts—is normal. Pursuing sales is tough since it can mean getting frequent rejections! But if that anxiety is feeling more like fear, do some self reflection to see if your motivations are for the best interest of the prospect.

Another side of the fear equation is the fear of approaching new people or markets. So we may keep mining the same group of old contacts, over and over again. It is true that existing customers and contacts can be some of the best prospects for new sales. But there does come a point when those markets have become saturated. Time to move on.

Ways to Properly Update Old Colleagues and Friends

Say there is some valid sales potential in a group of old friends and colleagues. What are some ways to approach them in a more transparent or less aggressive way?

Keep in Touch Consistently. Maybe it's a holiday card or email with an annual "here's what's happening here" message. No matter what holiday it's sent for, the point is that it's done EVERY year. Even better is to have a regular "keep in touch" email marketing or direct mail plan in force all year long.

Mail or Email Official Announcements. Mailed and emailed announcements are so much less intrusive than phone calls to announce job changes, new products, services and projects.

Keep LinkedIn Profile Updated. LinkedIn, with its more professional focus, should be updated as soon as career or business changes occur. Connections who elect to receive updates about changes in their network will often get these notices via email.

CHAPTER 16:

Phone Etiquette for Leaving Messages When Making Networking Outreach Calls

While I used to write about using mobile phones and technology, I have to confess that I really hate getting certain types of phone calls. More specifically, I HATE getting this type of call:

> *"Hi, this is _____ from _____, call me at ____ when you get a chance. Bye."*

It's bad enough when you get those types of calls from family and friends or when those two blanks are filled with a person's name and company that you recognize. It's worse when you have no idea who the person or company is.

And one thing is guaranteed. I will NOT be calling this person back. These calls violate principles of good business phone etiquette. Let's see how...

The 5 Biggest Problems with Cryptic Callers

So what's wrong with that message? Well, it's...

Presumptuous. Unless you have a continuing relationship going on, to leave a message like that above presumes a relationship that may not exist.

Fearful. Sometimes when people just leave a "call me" message, they have some information or a request that they feel will not be well received. So if you don't answer right away, they'll just leave their contact information to lull themselves into feeling good about themselves. They "tried."

Manipulative. The worst case instance of this is when the caller knows that when the person called sees his name or where he is from, it will automatically bring up either curiosity or be troubling, almost guaranteeing a call back. I've received just this type of call from a very large business rating organization (who I won't name here) some years ago. The first time it happened, I was disturbed. What could they be calling about? Did I get reported for something? (It was hard for me to imagine any of my customers going that route.) So I called back (and, of course, played voicemail tag for a couple days). Why did they call? They had run across one of my websites and wanted to sell me membership in their organization for several hundred dollars. Unbelievable! I have ignored all subsequent calls from this organization.

"We've Got to Talk." Ugh! If the tone used when a significant other, parent, friend, colleague, vendor or client suggests "we've got to talk," the possibilities of "what's wrong" will run rampant through the head of the person being called. It's a variation on the manipulative behavior just discussed, but this one packs an additional emotional wallop.

"Call Me" Phone Etiquette

Are there going to be situations where you need to leave a "call me" message for someone? Sure. But there's a way to do it to encourage people to return your calls by making it a safe communicating zone.

Here's a simple script to try:

"Hi, this is _____ from _____ and my number is _____. I'm calling about _____. Again, this is _____ from _____. The best time to reach me is _____ and my number is _____. Thanks much!"

The most important part of this is the ***"I'm calling about_____."*** Even if it's something tough that needs to be addressed, at least the person being called knows why you're connecting and they'll be better prepared to discuss the issue.

Also notice that the name and phone number are said twice. Why? When someone is listening to a phone message, they may miss the number when it's first said or may get only part of it. Stating it again at the end makes it easy for them to get your number by listening to the message only once. So you're not wasting their time which will be appreciated.

One other tip following up on the last point: Speak clearly. There is nothing more frustrating than trying to catch a phone number that's garbled. Granted, with the rise of Caller ID and smartphones which display callers' numbers, some of this isn't as big of a deal as it once was. However, if you're calling someone from an alternate phone line that you don't want the person to use to connect, indicating the best number to reach you is still a best practice to follow.

Another important segment of the message is the ***"The best time to reach me is___."*** This helps cut down on the phone tag. Contrast this with the first bad example in this article. The caller said to call "when you get a chance." Guess what, if I receive the message, I may never get a chance to call back. Offering an ideal time to chat can help increase the chances that you'll connect.

The Call Back

Just for grins, I actually called back on one of those cryptic messages. What did the caller want? To pick my brain. Guess I could have predicted that.

CHAPTER 17:
Are You Following Up or Fouling Up?

Persistent or Pest?

Went to a business lunch where people in my industry were invited to chat about sales and marketing. At the event, one gentleman told the story of how he called on a prospective client every month for something like three years before they became a customer. If it was a monthly call, that's around 36 calls. And these calls apparently were in person.

Follow up, the process of connecting and moving the sales process closer to a close, is a necessary element of selling success. However, many people follow up so much, or in such an annoying manner, that they are actually fouling up and driving away sales.

Grinding away at getting prospects to buy may have worked in the past. But not now. Interestingly, though the sales landscape has changed quite dramatically over the years, ineffective follow up tactics have not. Here's what's happening...

7 Fouled Up Follow Up Sins

Here are some common ways people foul up as they proceed through the selling process with customers:

"Did You Forget About Me?" These intrepid people call or email the customer over and over again, hoping that on the next contact the customer will magically say yes. In the back of their minds, they're thinking that customers may have just forgotten about them or their offer. In reality, that is probably true. People are overwhelmed at home and the job. But here's the kicker: If customers are really interested, they don't forget even if they don't act right away. So if a salesperson's presentation or offer is forgotten, it probably isn't compelling enough for prospects to make a buying decision. Emotionally, that is a tough fact for many in sales to swallow. Time to forget the forgetters and move on.

Not Properly Qualifying. Not being able to qualify the tire kickers from the truly qualified causes many to incessantly follow up with all the wrong leads that are going nowhere.

Presuming All Sales are Good Sales. Some people cling to every sales lead, regardless if it is one that is impossible to service or not. They've presumed that any and all sales are good sales. So they drone on with their never-ending follow up, chasing business that they'd be better off leaving behind.

Just Making the Numbers. Others really don't care whether a sale closes or not. They just need to make the required number of sales lead follow up calls to meet their quota (even if it's an arbitrary self-imposed one).

Not Talking to the Real Decisionmaker. Similar to those who cannot distinguish the qualified from unqualified leads, some people slog through a pool of contacts, none of which has any decisionmaking authority. They'll contact these folks over and over again, hoping that one day they'll get introduced to the check signing bigwigs. What they fail (or refuse) to recognize is that these useless contacts are the gatekeepers, keeping the sales riffraff from getting through. What often trips up these people is that the gatekeepers may give the impression that they have more authority than they really do.

Busy Work. Unproductive follow up activities can make salespeople feel like they're doing something. But in sales, all that matters is making sales. Time to quit following up on leads that aren't closing and look for some greener pastures (the cash greener kind).

Unable to Identify Customer Signals. Some clueless people just can't read customers buying—or non-buying—signals. So they keep up their fruitless quest of dead or dying leads.

Why People Foul Up

If these behaviors are so annoying, why do people act this way? One big reason: Fear. Fear of what?

Fear of Losing Sales. This is obvious. They're afraid of not making their numbers or being unsuccessful. So they keep hammering away at the leads they have, even though they might be better advised to find more profitable and productive prospects.

Fear of Losing Control of the Sale. After people make their best offers and presentations, the sales process is out of their control and is in the customer's court. This is a painful reality for many. So to feel like they're still in control, they incessantly hound every lead they get until customers either quit communicating with them or give in to the sale in hopes of making them go away. Note the term "give in," not "buy in."

Tips for Ditching the Follow up Frenzy

To help keep follow up from driving both you and your customers crazy, keep these tips in mind:

Ask What's Appropriate. If an offer is made and the sale is not closed immediately, the sales process is really in the customer's court. Ask the customer what would be an appropriate follow up interval to check on progress. Also confirm customer's preferred method of follow up, whether that be a meeting, phone call or email. For online sales, this would most likely be entirely completed via email. Then keep to the plan and follow up!

Decide When to Quit Following. Some leads will just not close for a variety of reasons, even after proper qualification and follow up are done. Make a decision at what point a sales lead will be considered dead. This could be after a certain time interval or after a specific number of follow up efforts. Chasing leads that will not close wastes time and can erode a company's sales and profit picture.

Find a Way to Keep in Touch with Qualified Leads who are Not Ready to Buy Right Now. There are some prospects that are ideal, but just aren't currently in a position to pull the trigger on a sale. For these qualified prospects, keep in contact in less aggressive ways such as email marketing, social media or direct mail. This keeps you and your brand in top of mind awareness for when they are ready to buy.

CHAPTER 18:
Are You Selling the Impossible?

Had a revelation about my business that can have a profound effect on profitability, productivity and sales. When I was in the promotional product business, I had access to no less than 3,000 different suppliers and over half a million product SKUs. The temptation to use any or all of them was strong, make that STRONG. And here's the scenario that could have gotten me into trouble.

A customer had a "vision" for an upcoming project. I would show him the possibilities that I had as standard offerings through my online shopsites or from my preferred supply chain partners. Um, didn't quite match the unrealistic dream. Then the wild goose chase began!

Database research, calling suppliers, checking catalogs... I could have been putting in hours of work and the sale hadn't even closed yet. Compounding the issue was that a quantity of only 500, maybe even 50, was needed. May sound like a big quantity for a small, solopreneur business. But in the promotional products world, that's usually a small order. Then, after the whole research process, I often got THAT email, the one that said, *"Thanks for your help, but we've decided to [go with another supplier, scrap/postpone the project, not spend the money or some lame excuse]."*

Being concerned about customer service, in the past I would often chase these impossible inquiries (emphasis on "in the past"). But was that really service? Or was I providing these off-the-menu choices out of fear of losing sales and the opportunity to serve?

Then when I got older and wiser, I would send these folks to one of my knowledgeable competitors who could do the project better than I ever could.

Let's look a little deeper at why this type of scenario happens in small businesses...

Like Ford Selling Chevys

Solopreneurs and self-employed folks have to remember the scenario discussed above is like Ford selling Chevys. Ludicrous notion, of course. Except for the sales of used cars of many makes, auto dealers would NEVER entertain the impossible inquiry of a customer who wandered into the dealership asking to buy a new car from a competing manufacturer. Not only would it be detrimental to their brand to offer it, it would cost them more to service this business, too.

Contrast this to small businesses who can be ridiculously prone to taking on impossible projects that are "not in their wheelhouse." If it is so obvious to most bigger businesses, why do the little guys do this?

Fear of Losing Sales. In the early years, especially for consulting or extreme niche operations, sales can be few and far between. So they latch on to any inquiry that happens to wander in. They end up reinventing the business to meet every single customer demand.

Feeling Like a Superhero... or Want to Appear So.
Ever see the contractor trucks that say "Residential, Commercial and Industrial?" Anyone who has a good understanding of the contracting business knows that serving individual consumers is completely different than dealing with commercial and industrial facility managers. A variation on this theme are the consultants who say they work with "small businesses to Fortune 100 clients." Some newbie consultants, particularly those that have come from a corporate background, have an understanding of doing business within large operations. But when they go into business for themselves, they don't feel they have a prayer of getting sales from big businesses (and they may be right). So they take a stab at doing business with individual consumers or other customers out of their comfort and experience zone. Then they get a huge dose of culture shock when they sell in the B2C (business to consumer) and may even give up to go back to a "real job."

Who Are You and Who Are Your Customers?
Solopreneurs and consultants who say they serve everybody, don't know who or what they are. Even worse is that they don't know who or what their customers are either. So every inquiry, even the impossible ones, are pursued. They're just hoping that at least some of them will close.

How to Avoid Doing the Impossible

While networking, you may be the closest thing to what a connection wants or needs. Even though you don't have the ability or capacity to serve them, they reach out to you anyway. Being a friendly networker, you want to help them. But taking on projects or sales that are impossible for you to handle damages your reputation.

Avoiding getting trapped in impossible selling scenarios requires a thorough understanding of your business, its capabilities and limitations:

Nosce Te Ipsum (Know Thyself). Take an inventory of skills, products and services that can be effectively AND cost effectively provided. Be specific to the Nth degree! If the overall skill is marketing, what kind of marketing tasks can be offered? There are probably hundreds of niches to fill in the marketing arena.

Define Customers. Who are those customers that need the products and services that can be offered? Don't say "everybody!" Define the folks by industry, job title, hobbies, age, gender... using several marketing demographic factors helps focus sales and marketing efforts.

Develop a "Menu" of Products and Services... and Stick to It! On the popular restaurant makeover reality shows, one of the common problems plaguing the troubled operations is a bloated menu, sometimes spanning several pages. The inventory, chef skill and marketing of these extensive offerings can cripple the business. But no matter what industry a business is in, all need to develop a "menu" of standard products and services to be offered. This streamlines the operation and focuses marketing and sales efforts. Sticking to this standard menu will turn away some high maintenance customers (see discussions of "off the menu" offerings below). But the meager benefits to be gained from these will almost always not be worth the effort and cost.

Develop a Standard of Service. In addition to the "what" on a menu of products and services, a "how" should also be developed for their delivery. That could mean delivery only by a carrier such as UPS, pickup only in stores, restricting acceptance of orders to online or by phone, limiting sales territory, etc. The cost to deliver goods and services needs to be built into the pricing structure and profit margin projections. **Example:** Some prospects wanted to chat about their promotions with me in their offices. Sorry, folks, that's consulting and it was too expensive for me to chase these types of requests that almost inevitably result in a measly order of a couple hundred bucks or even one of those "we bought from someone else" emails. (Had it happen too many times!) That's why I developed extensive shopsites they could browse through on their time and dime.

Develop Premium Pricing and Justification for "Off the Menu" Choices. Granted, taking on some impossible projects can help a company stretch its capabilities. But as a daily occurrence, it will drain resources. So if a company wants to offer some "off the menu" products and services, premium higher pricing and/or justification for these offerings needs to be established. **Example #1:** In my previous promotional business, I offered a couple of online shopsites featuring hundreds upon hundreds of different items each. If a customer or prospect could not find a solution within this wide selection, I charged a hefty fee to do a custom search, even if the sale did not close. Often that ended the discussion OR they discovered a standard offering that will suffice. This weeded out the tire kickers. **Example #2:** I received an inquiry to do promotions for a television show. While I didn't charge premium prices, I did justify accepting it with the goal of learning about the "off MY menu" entertainment industry to see if it was worth pursuing in the future.

Refer Impossible Business to Appropriate Competitors and Allied Businesses. Developing a network of friendly and competent competitors and allied businesses is also key to eliminating doing impossible business. As soon as an inquiry that doesn't meet the standard customer profile is received, it should be evaluated for referral to other networking colleagues that could handle it more appropriately. You as the referring business also win by looking like a well-connected and knowledgeable businessperson.

CHAPTER 19:
Preventing Brain Picking When Networking

Consultants, Beware!

Say you're a consultant (or coach) and your networking 1:1 (one-to-one) meeting with a new connection is going great. You're chatting about your shared affinity for a favorite pop star, where you went to college, your crazy pets, that new restaurant in the area and, of course, what you do for work. Your new pal starts talking about some of the challenges she's facing in her business. And then, here it comes...

"I'd like to pick your brain about..."
OR
"What do you think I should do about..."
OR
"I'm working on ___, could you just take a look at this and see what you think?"

Ugh! You've just walked into a brain picking! This scenario is all too familiar for those in the consulting professions. I can't tell you how many billable hours I've forfeited due to being brain picked! Many people cannot distinguish between what's friendly conversation and what's consulting or coaching. Even worse is that consultants often don't know how to politely respond to these requests for input, whether they occur on the phone or in an in-person meeting as the one described above. They're afraid of hurting the other person who could be a potential client. So they usually cave in and comply.

From another perspective, the networker asking for advice has not officially hired the consultant. So is the consultant liable for any advice given?

Creating Boundaries and Possibilities for Brain Picks

As a consultant active in the networking scene, you will likely receive invitations for coffee, meals or phone meetings with new connections. These meetings can be very important for building rapport with potential clients and referral partners. So, yes, accept invitations from those you feel could be relevant connections.

From my experience, these meetings are usually very enjoyable and deepen important friendships. But you need to be extremely vigilant and listen carefully for statements like those highlighted at the beginning of the chapter. When they occur, you need to sidestep answering and suggest that those issues be addressed in a separate (PAID, we hope!) session dedicated to addressing the person's needs. Best way to be ready is to have a response script prepared and practiced.

Brain Pick Script Elements
- *Acknowledge the person's need and the importance of addressing it.*
- *Stress that limited time and attention exists in the current "networking" meeting.*

- *Invite to a paid consulting session. Indicating how much it will cost can help ease their minds. Alternatively, if you offer a free initial assessment or consult, invite them to book it so that you can get them into your sales funnel.*

Example:

> *"That's an important issue that could really affect the future of your business* [health, family or whatever the issue is]. *Since we have limited time in our networking meetup today, let's plan to dedicate some time to your issue in a consulting session. I charge $* [insert details on costs and booking]. *Should we take a look at our calendars and book that session now?"*

You may find that interjecting an offer like this—and setting a healthy boundary—may completely disarm your network buddies. They may decline your offer initially, but will likely keep it in the back of their minds. Or they may feel that you are opportunistic, selfish, etc. That's THEIR problem! But you'll have planted a seed that:

- *You have knowledge, skill and experience to address their concerns; and,*
- *Your time and talent are valuable... and that you respect their time, too.*

Brain Pick Redirect: Referral to a Networking Colleague

If you cannot address these people's concerns, that's fine. And you don't want to stress out your brain trying to find an answer that you don't have, especially in the short period of time in a networking meeting. As discussed in the earlier chapter on selling the impossible, you are much better off referring inappropriate opportunities to another networking connection who can help. In that case, the script would be altered a bit:

Brain Pick Script Elements for a Referral

- *Acknowledge the person's need and the importance of addressing it*
- *Indicate that you don't have the skills, experience, etc. to competently address their needs.*
- *Ask if they would be interested in being referred to one of your colleagues.*

Example:
> *"That's an important issue that could really affect the future of your business* [health, family or whatever the issue is]. *However, since I specialize in* [insert your specialty here], *I'm probably not the best person to talk to about this. Would you mind if I refer you to a colleague of mine who's better qualified?"*

You'll look like a well-connected professional and your network pal can get the help they really need. I've successfully done this on a number of occasions!

MEASURING YOUR NETWORKING SUCCESS

CHAPTER 20:
How to Measure If Your Networking is Working

I Was Exhausted!

As social media began to become THE way to network, I embraced it totally. At the same time, I was also networking IRL (in real life) like crazy. Chambers, events, leads groups, lots of 1:1 (one-to-one) meetings... you name it. I was getting recognition, but getting exhausted, too. And my financials weren't painting a good picture, in spite of my efforts.

So that's when I sought out some professional help and hired a business coach. And that's when I learned how to more accurately measure my networking success. As discussed in the earlier chapter, *"Types of Networking Groups,"* not all networking venues are equal in terms of the opportunities they offer.

Here are some of the things I learned from my analysis...

How Should Networking Results be Measured?

This is one of the toughest topics! While you could do some super sophisticated analysis of interactions, events, etc. (yes, I've done some of that and it's a project!), that is usually beyond what most solopreneurs and self-employed consultants are willing to do. So to get a rough idea of what's working and what's not, you need to track some simple metrics over time:

Number of Activities by Group. These could be either offline or online or both.

Amount of Time Spent in Each Group. This will be an eye-opener! Don't just track the amount of time for the actual event or meeting. Add the amount of prep, travel and recovery (yes, recovery!) time needed. This additional time can balloon your networking time exponentially.

Number of Referrals Received from Each Group. These are genuine connections and introductions sent your way by someone else.

Number of Referrals Given to Each Group. A good metric to determine if you're contributing or are able to contribute. You may want to include your purchases from network members. But if almost all of your referrals are your personal purchases, that's a red flag since it can mean that your personal pool of contacts is not very deep or relevant. Or it can mean that the people in the group have nothing to offer the people you know. Either way, it can signal a bad fit.

Number of Sales Made from Each Group. The actual total number of transactions you complete.

Total Dollar Value of Sales from Each Group. Your total sales revenues, apportioned by group source.

Number of Direct Visits to Your Website. This number can be found in Google Analytics. The program logs how many people actually type in your website's address direct into their browser. This can be a pretty good measure of people who have seen or received your information, business card, press about you, etc. and typed in your web address to learn more.

Number of Visits to Your Website from Social Media Networks. Google Analytics has a breakdown of visits your site receives from social media. Really helpful to figure out if all those tweets and posts are generating any web traffic.

Analyzing Networking Numbers

Each of the metrics discussed above must be time bound, for example, for the calendar year, this fiscal quarter, etc. Be aware that to gain more accurate trends, these metrics must be measured and monitored over an extended period of time (minimum of one year).

While you could get pretty detailed in how you analyze your networking metrics, keep it simple. Below are just six of the ways you could evaluate your numbers. There could be other important comparisons, too. Pick those that are most relevant for you, but do pick at least a few analyses to make an accurate assessment.

- ***Number of Activities by Group to Number of Sales Made from Each Group.*** Where the rubber meets the road! Evaluates whether your networking is working.
- ***Number of Activities by Group to Number of Referrals Received from Each Group.*** Like comparing activities to sales, this provides a good measure of how active and valuable the

connections you're making are. If your referral level is low, might be time to reevaluate your networking groups and activities.

- **Number of Referrals Received from Each Group to Number of Sales Made from Each Group.** Evaluates the quality of the referrals you're receiving.

- **Number of Referrals Received from Each Group to Total Dollar Value of Sales Made from Group.** Evaluates whether the referrals you're receiving are worth anything. You could be getting a lot of low dollar value business that increases your workload. It often takes just as long to manage a low dollar sale as it does for a bigger one. Good metric of the efficiency of your activities.

- **Total Number of Activities Completed to Total Dollar Value of Sales Made.** You'll get an idea of how much personal effort it could take to generate a certain sales volume.

- **Number of Activities by Group to Number of Referrals Given to Each Group.** This is a good metric of whether you're a good fit for the people in your network. Remember, networking is a two-way street.

A standard spreadsheet type program (such as Microsoft Excel) can be used to build these analyses. Here's an example...

Group	Number of Activities	Number of Referrals Received
Networking Group #1	6	0
Networking Group #2	3	5
Networking Group #3	4	1
TOTAL	13	6

The example analysis could suggest that over the time period being analyzed: a) It took 13 activities to generate 6 referrals; b) Group #1 might be a time waster; and, c) Group #2 might warrant more attention.

Don't Jump to Conclusions

CAUTION! Avoid the temptation to expect networking events results immediately or even within the immediate time period, such as this quarter. You're looking for long term trends.

For example, you log a certain number of networking events in this quarter and a certain number of sales or referrals. But don't think that the events in this quarter were the exact ones that generated those results. The event you attended 6 or even 12 months ago may have generated the sale you made today. So when beginning to track these stats, give it at least 6 to 12 months before deciding that this or that networking activity or group isn't working. It takes time to build the trust and relationships needed to do business.

As Your Business Changes, So Do Your Networks

What networking activities and groups worked this year may be totally irrelevant next year... especially if your business has changed.

In one year, I dropped two networking groups in which I had been very active just because my business changed. These groups could no longer provide the types of referrals and sales I needed to grow.

It was a tough choice since I did genuinely like the people in these groups and some had become friends. But only through doing analyses like those discussed here was I able to emotionally muster up the courage to make a stand for my future and finances by letting go.

How Often Should These Stats be Tracked and Tallied?

While it will depend on how active the business is on a daily basis, for small businesses, tracking activity and sales results achieved every week—or monthly at minimum—is usually sufficient help keep things on track. Then analyze monthly, quarterly and annually.

GOING FORWARD

CHAPTER 21:
Add Heidi to Your Network!

Dr. Heidi Thorne, MBA/DBA, is an author and business speaker who focuses on small business and marketing topics. She has over 25 years of experience in sales, advertising, marketing and public relations, including a decade in the hospitality and trade show industries. As well, she was a trade newspaper editor for over 15 years, has blogged since 2010 and taught at the college level for five years.

Books. Heidi has written several books and eBooks on business and self publishing. For a current listing of all books, with links to purchase, visit the "Books" page at HeidiThorne.com.

Speaking. Need a speaker for your business event? Let Heidi engage and entertain your audience! For video previews and current topics, visit the "Speaking" page at HeidiThorne.com.